3-CHORD CHRISTMAS CAROLS FOR UKULELE

ISBN 978-1-4768-1252-6

HAL•LEONARD®
CORPORATION
7777 W. BLUEMOUND RD. P.O. BOX 13819 MILWAUKEE, WI 53213

In Australia Contact:
Hal Leonard Australia Pty. Ltd.
4 Lentara Court
Cheltenham, Victoria, 3192 Australia
Email: ausadmin@halleonard.com.au

For all works contained herein:
Unauthorized copying, arranging, adapting, recording, Internet posting, public performance,
or other distribution of the printed music in this publication is an infringement of copyright.
Infringers are liable under the law.

Visit Hal Leonard Online at
www.halleonard.com

CONTENTS

Angels We Have Heard on High

Traditional French Carol
Translated by James Chadwick

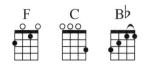

First note

Verse
Joyfully

1. An - gels we have heard on high
2. Shep - herds, why this ju - bi - lee?
3. Come to Beth - le - hem and see
4. See with - in a man - ger laid

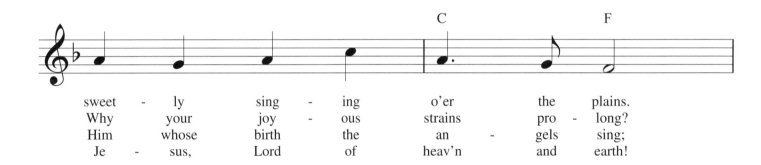

sweet - ly sing - ing o'er the plains.
Why your joy - ous strains pro - long?
Him whose birth the an - gels sing;
Je - sus, Lord of heav'n and earth!

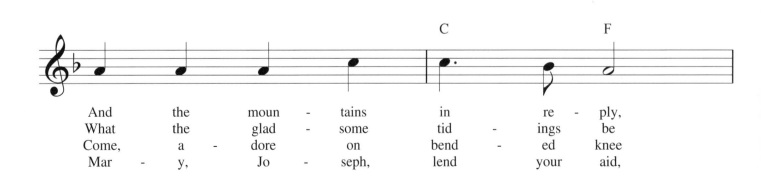

And the moun - tains in re - ply,
What the glad - some tid - ings be
Come, a - dore on bend - ed knee
Mar - y, Jo - seph, lend your aid,

Copyright © 2012 by HAL LEONARD CORPORATION
International Copyright Secured   All Rights Reserved

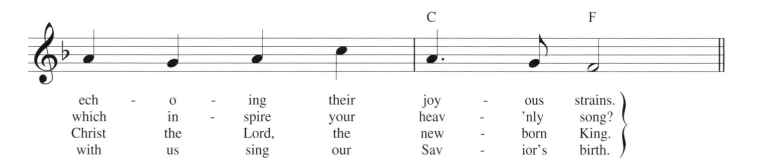

ech - o - ing their joy - ous strains.
which in - spire your heav - 'nly song?
Christ the Lord, the new - born King.
with us sing our Sav - ior's birth.

Chorus

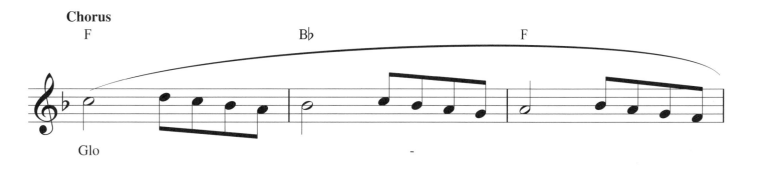

Glo -

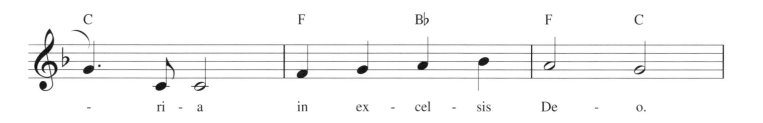

-ri - a in ex - cel - sis De - o.

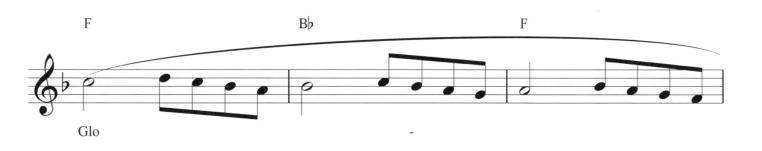

Glo -

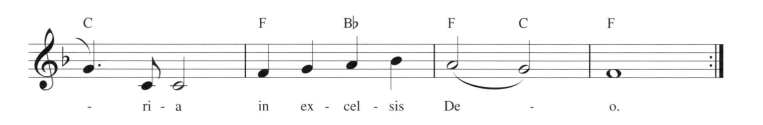

-ri - a in ex - cel - sis De - o.

Away in a Manger

Anonymous Text (vv. 1, 2)
Text by John T. McFarland (v. 3)
Music by James R. Murray

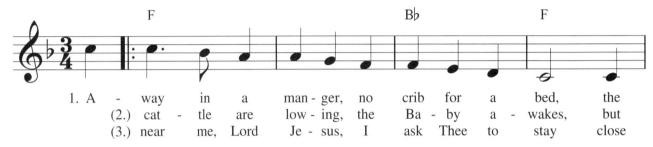

First note

Verse
Sweetly

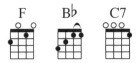

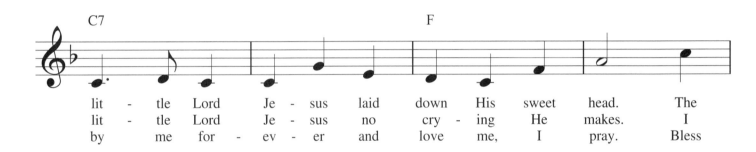

1. A - way in a man - ger, no crib for a bed, the
(2.) cat - tle are low - ing, the Ba - by a - wakes, but
(3.) near me, Lord Je - sus, I ask Thee to stay close

lit - tle Lord Je - sus laid down His sweet head. The
lit - tle Lord Je - sus no cry - ing He makes. I
by me for - ev - er and love me, I pray. Bless

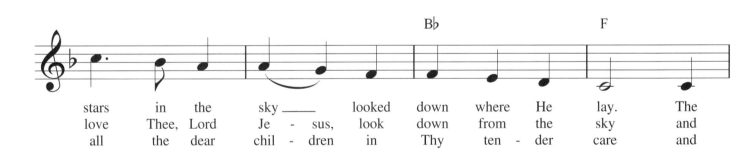

stars in the sky ___ looked down where He lay. The
love Thee, Lord Je - sus, look down from the sky and
all the dear chil - dren in Thy ten - der care and

lit - tle Lord Je - sus, a - sleep on the hay. 2. The
stay by my cra - dle 'til morn - ing is nigh. 3. Be
fit us for heav - en to live with Thee there.

Copyright © 2012 by HAL LEONARD CORPORATION
International Copyright Secured   All Rights Reserved

Ding Dong! Merrily on High!

Traditional French Carol

First note

G C D7

Verse
Joyfully

1. Ding dong! Mer - ri - ly on high in heav'n the bells are
2., 3. *See additional lyrics*

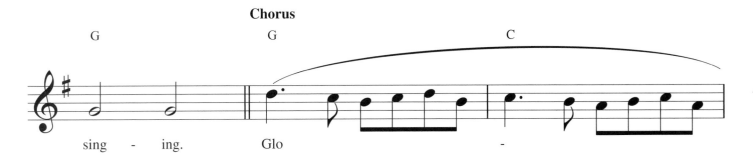

ring - ing. Ding dong! Ver - i - ly the sky is riv'n with an - gel

Chorus

sing - ing. Glo - -

- ri - a, Ho - san - na in ex - cel - sis!

Additional Lyrics

2. E'en so here below, below, let steeple bells be swinging.
And i-o, i-o, i-o, by priest and people singing.

3. Pray you, dutifully prime your matin chime, ye ringers.
May you beautiful rime your evetime song, ye singers.

Copyright © 2012 by HAL LEONARD CORPORATION
International Copyright Secured All Rights reserved

Bring a Torch, Jeannette, Isabella

17th Century French Provençal Carol

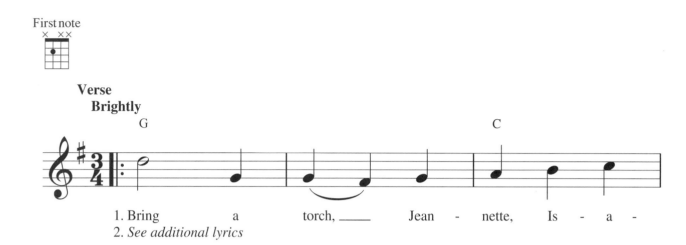

First note

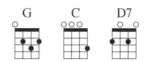

Verse
Brightly

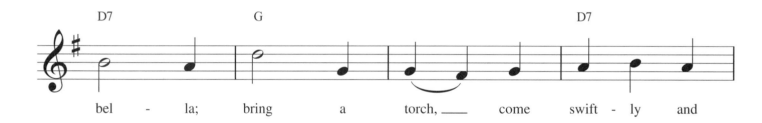

1. Bring a torch, ____ Jean - nette, Is - a -
2. *See additional lyrics*

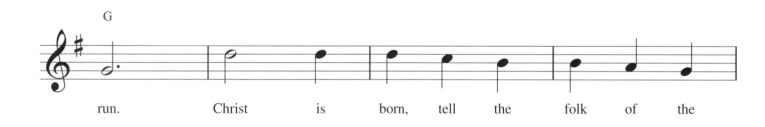

bel - la; bring a torch, ____ come swift - ly and

run. Christ is born, tell the folk of the

vil - lage, Je - sus is sleep - ing in His

Copyright © 2012 by HAL LEONARD CORPORATION
International Copyright Secured   All Rights Reserved

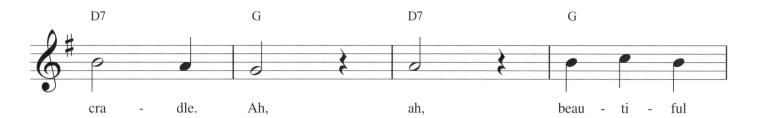

cra - dle. Ah, ah, beau - ti - ful

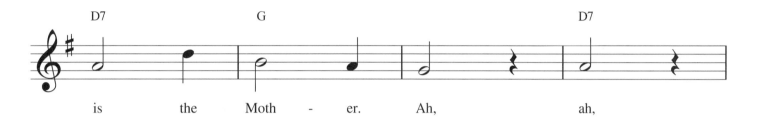

is the Moth - er. Ah, ah,

beau - ti - ful is her Son. _____

Additional Lyrics

2. Hasten now, good folk of the village,
Hasten now, the Christ Child to see.
You will find Him asleep in a manger,
Quietly come and whisper softly.
Hush, hush, peacefully now He slumbers,
Hush, hush, peacefully now He sleeps.

Come, Thou Long-Expected Jesus

Words by Charles Wesley
Music by Rowland Hugh Prichard

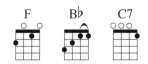

First note

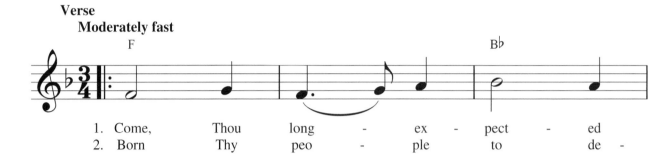

Verse
Moderately fast

1. Come, Thou long - ex - pect - ed
2. Born Thy peo - ple to de -

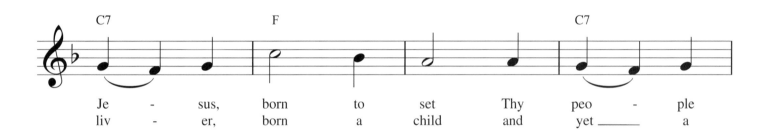

Je - sus, born to set Thy peo - ple
liv - er, born a child and yet ____ a

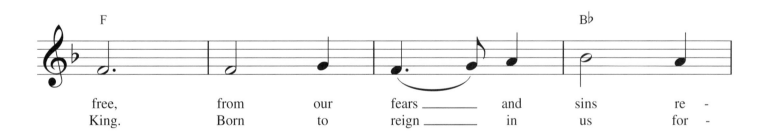

free, from our fears ____ and sins re -
King. Born to reign ____ in us for -

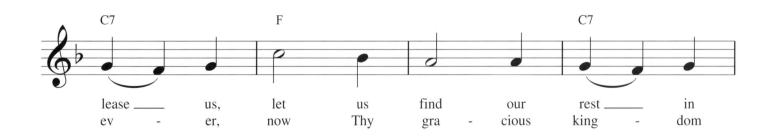

lease ____ us, let us find our rest ____ in
ev - er, now Thy gra - cious king - dom

Copyright © 2012 by HAL LEONARD CORPORATION
International Copyright Secured   All Rights Reserved

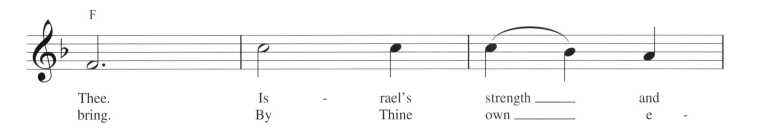

Thee.   Is - rael's   strength _____   and
bring.   By   Thine   own _____   e -

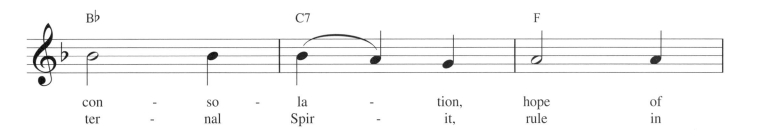

con - so - la - tion,   hope   of
ter - nal   Spir - it,   rule   in

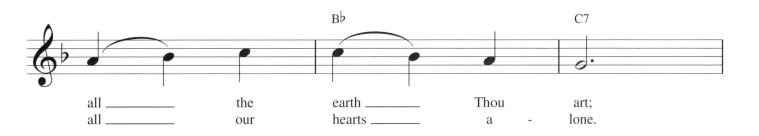

all _____   the   earth _____   Thou   art;
all _____   our   hearts _____   a - lone.

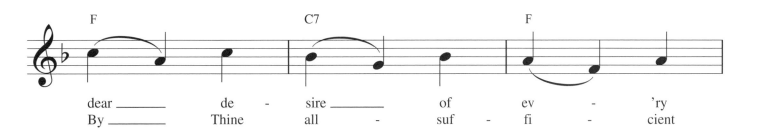

dear _____   de - sire _____   of   ev - 'ry
By _____   Thine   all - suf - fi - cient

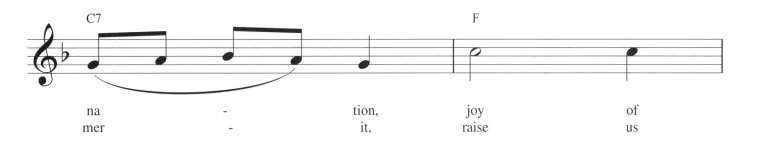

na - tion,   joy   of
mer - it,   raise   us

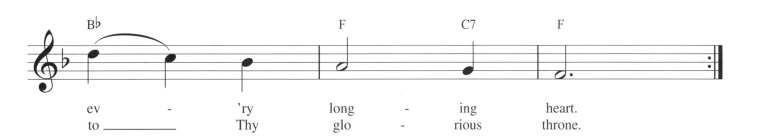

ev - 'ry   long - ing   heart.
to _____   Thy   glo - rious   throne.

Deck the Hall

Traditional Welsh Carol

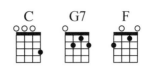

First note

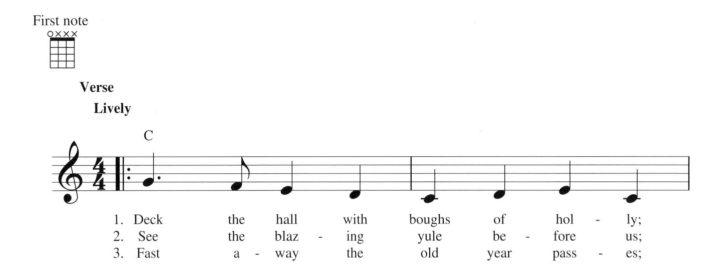

Verse
Lively

1. Deck the hall with boughs of hol - ly;
2. See the blaz - ing yule be - fore us;
3. Fast a - way the old year pass - es;

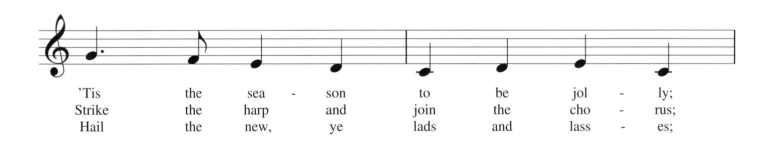

fa, la, la, la, la, la, la, la, la.
fa, la, la, la, la, la, la, la, la.
fa, la, la, la, la, la, la, la, la.

'Tis the sea - son to be jol - ly;
Strike the harp and join the cho - rus;
Hail the new, ye lads and lass - es;

fa, la, la, la, la, la, la, la, la.
fa, la, la, la, la, la, la, la, la.
fa, la, la, la, la, la, la, la, la.

Copyright © 2012 by HAL LEONARD CORPORATION
International Copyright Secured   All Rights Reserved

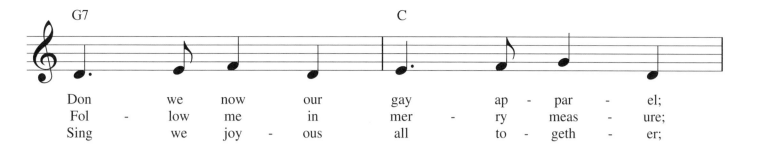

Don we now our gay ap - par - el;
Fol - low me in mer - ry meas - ure;
Sing we joy - ous all to - geth - er;

fa, la, la, la, la, la, la, la, la.
fa, la, la, la, la, la, la, la, la.
fa, la, la, la, la, la, la, la, la.

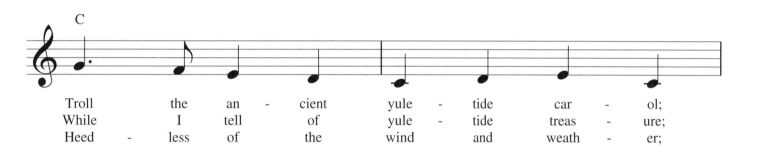

Troll the an - cient yule - tide car - ol;
While I tell of yule - tide treas - ure;
Heed - less of the wind and weath - er;

fa, la, la, la, la, la, la, la, la.
fa, la, la, la, la, la, la, la, la.
fa, la, la, la, la, la, la, la, la.

The First Noel

17th Century English Carol
Music from W. Sandys' *Christmas Carols*

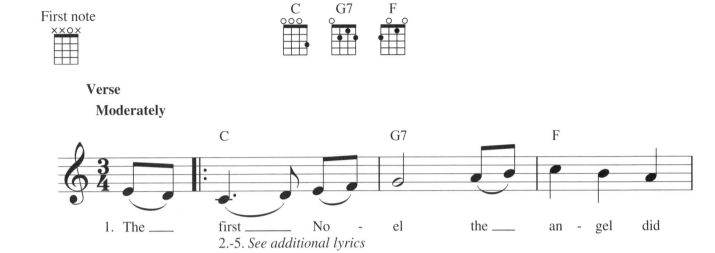

Verse

Moderately

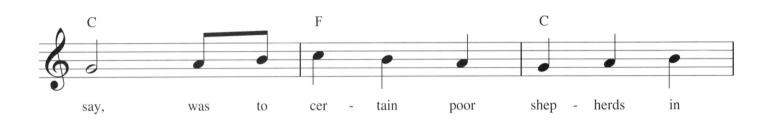

1. The ___ first _____ No - el the ___ an - gel did
2.-5. *See additional lyrics*

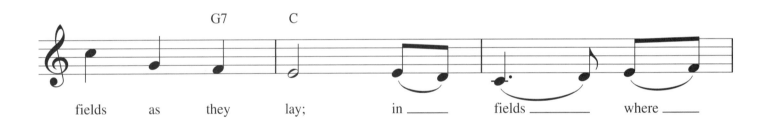

say,   was   to   cer - tain   poor   shep - herds   in

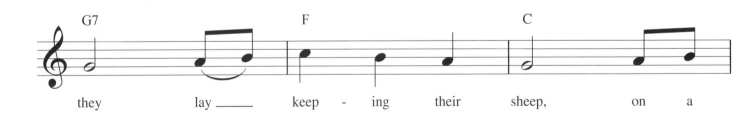

fields   as   they   lay;   in ___   fields _____   where ___

they   lay ___   keep - ing   their   sheep,   on   a

cold   win - ter's   night ___   that   was ___   so   deep.   No -

Copyright © 2012 by HAL LEONARD CORPORATION
International Copyright Secured   All Rights Reserved

Chorus

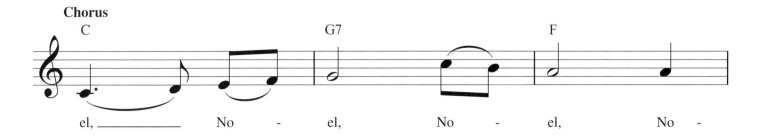

el, _____ No - el, No - el, No -

el, born is the King _____ of

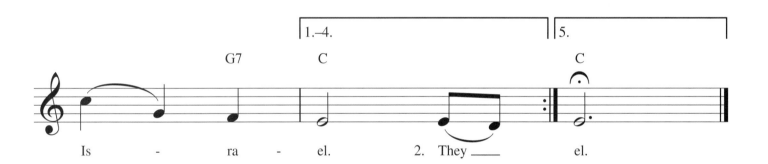

Is - ra - el. 2. They ____ el.

Additional Lyrics

2. They looked up and saw a star
   Shining in the east, beyond them far;
   And to the earth it gave great light
   And so it continued both day and night.

3. And by the light of that same star,
   Three wise men came from country far;
   To seek for a King was their intent,
   And to follow the star wherever it went.

4. This star drew nigh to the northwest,
   O'er Bethlehem it took its rest;
   And there it did both stop and stay,
   Right over the place where Jesus lay.

5. Then entered in those wise men three,
   Full reverently upon their knee;
   And offered there in His presence,
   Their gold and myrrh and frankincense.

The Friendly Beasts

Traditional English Carol

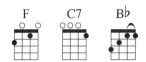

First note

Verse
Tenderly

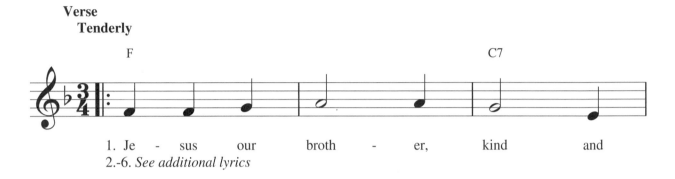

1. Je - sus   our   broth - er,   kind   and
2.-6. *See additional lyrics*

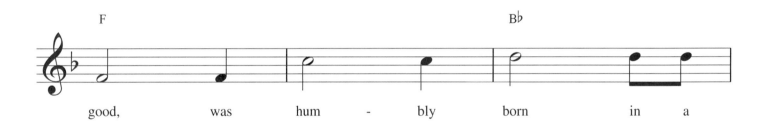

good,   was   hum - bly   born   in   a

sta - ble   rude;   and   the   friend - ly

Copyright © 2012 by HAL LEONARD CORPORATION
International Copyright Secured   All Rights Reserved

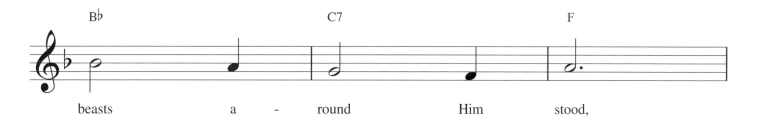

beasts   a - round   Him   stood,

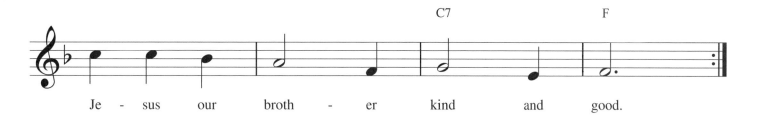

Je - sus our broth - er kind and good.

Additional Lyrics

2. "I," said the donkey, shaggy and brown,
   "I carried His mother up hill and down.
   I carried His mother to Bethlehem town."
   "I," said the donkey, shaggy and brown.

3. "I," said the cow, all white and red,
   "I gave Him my manger for His bed.
   I gave Him my hay to pillow His head."
   "I," said the cow, all white and red.

4. "I," said the sheep with the curly horn,
   "I gave Him my wool for His blanket warm.
   He wore my coat on Christmas morn."
   "I," said the sheep with the curly horn.

5. "I," said the dove from the rafters high,
   "I cooed Him to sleep that He would not cry.
   We cooed Him to sleep, my mate and I."
   "I," said the dove from the rafters high.

6. Thus every beast by some good spell,
   In the stable dark was glad to tell
   Of the gift he gave Emmanuel,
   The gift he gave Emmanuel.

Go, Tell It on the Mountain

African-American Spiritual
Verses by John W. Work, Jr.

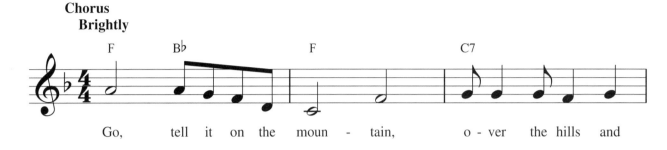

First note

Chorus
Brightly

Go, tell it on the moun - tain, o - ver the hills and

ev - 'ry - where. Go, tell it on the moun - tain that

Last time Fine
Verse

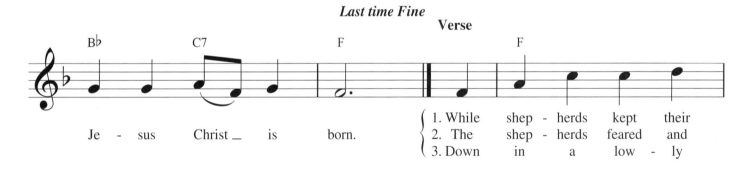

Je - sus Christ __ is born.

1. While shep - herds kept their
2. The shep - herds feared and
3. Down in a low - ly

watch - ing o'er si - lent flocks by night, be - hold! through - out the
trem - bled when, lo! a - bove the earth rang out the an - gel
man - ger the hum - ble Christ was born, and God sent us sal -

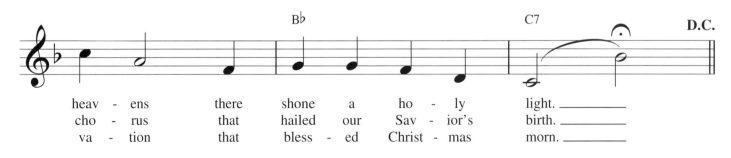

heav - ens there shone a ho - ly light. _____
cho - rus that hailed our Sav - ior's birth. _____
va - tion that bless - ed Christ - mas morn. _____

Copyright © 2012 by HAL LEONARD CORPORATION
International Copyright Secured   All Rights Reserved

I Heard the Bells on Christmas Day

Words by Henry Wadsworth Longfellow
Music by John Baptiste Calkin

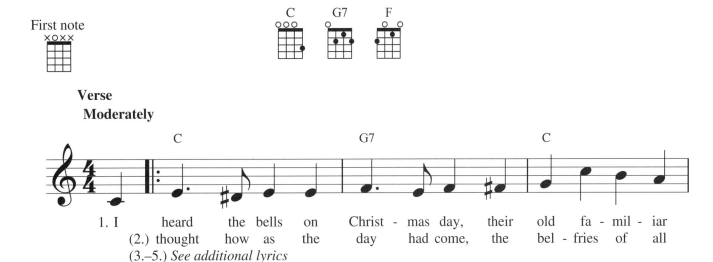

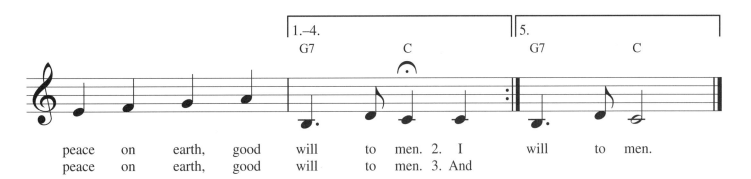

Additional Lyrics

3. And in despair I bowed my head:
   "There is no peace on earth," I said,
   "For hate is strong, and mocks the song
   Of peace on earth, good will to men."

4. Then pealed the bells more loud and deep:
   "God is not dead, nor doth He sleep;
   The wrong shall fail, the right prevail,
   With peace on earth, good will to men."

5. Till, ringing, singing on its way,
   The world revolved from night to day,
   A voice, a chime, a chant sublime,
   Of peace on earth, good will to men!

Copyright © 2012 by HAL LEONARD CORPORATION
International Copyright Secured   All Rights Reserved

God Rest Ye Merry, Gentlemen

19th Century English Carol

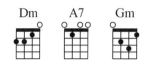

First note

Verse

Moderately, in 2

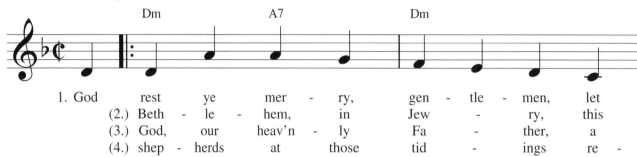

1. God rest ye mer - ry, gen - tle - men, let
(2.) Beth - le - hem, in Jew - ry, this
(3.) God, our heav'n - ly Fa - ther, a
(4.) shep - herds at those tid - ings re -

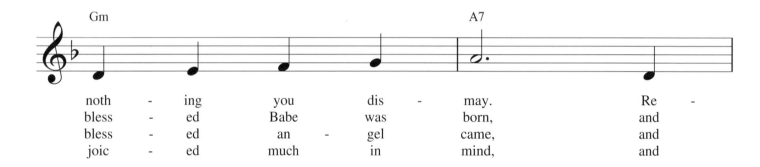

noth - ing you dis - may. Re -
bless - ed Babe was born, and
bless - ed an - gel came, and
joic - ed much in mind, and

mem - ber Christ, our Sav - ior, was
laid with - in a man - ger up -
un - to cer - tain shep - herds brought
left their flocks a - feed - ing in

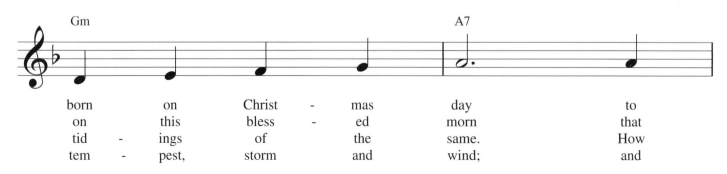

born on Christ - mas day to
on this bless - ed morn that
tid - ings of the same. How
tem - pest, storm and wind; and

Copyright © 2012 by HAL LEONARD CORPORATION
International Copyright Secured   All Rights Reserved

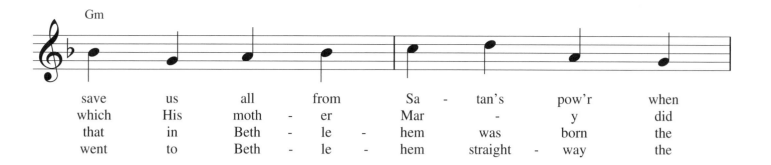

save us all from Sa - tan's pow'r when
which His moth - er Mar - y did
that in Beth - le - hem was born the
went to Beth - le - hem straight - way the

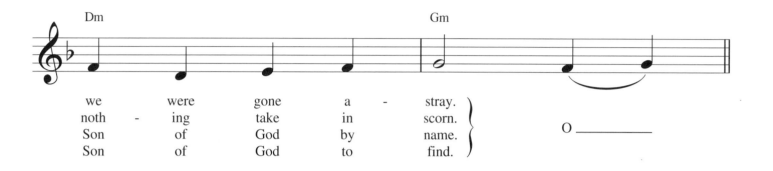

we were gone a - stray.
noth - ing take in scorn.
Son of God by name.
Son of God to find.
O _____

Chorus

tid - ings of com - fort and joy, com - fort and

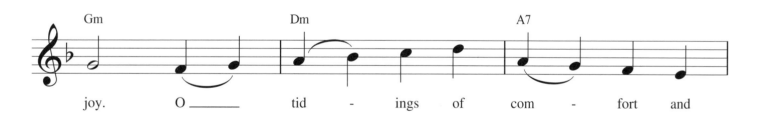

joy. O _____ tid - ings of com - fort and

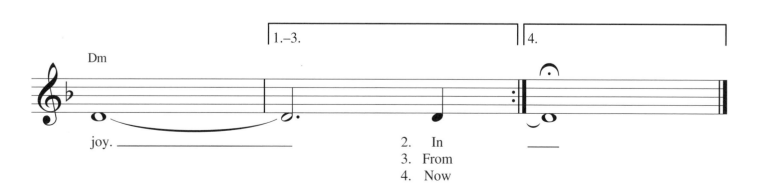

1.–3.   4.

joy. _____   2. In _____
3. From
4. Now

Good Christian Men, Rejoice

14th Century Latin Text
Translated by John Mason Neale
14th Century German Melody

First note

Verse
Brightly

1. Good Chris - tian men, re - joice _____ with heart and soul and
2., 3. *See additional lyrics*

voice. _____ Give ye heed to what we say:

News! News! Je - sus Christ is born to - day!

Ox and ass be - fore Him bow, and He is in the

Copyright © 2012 by HAL LEONARD CORPORATION
International Copyright Secured   All Rights Reserved

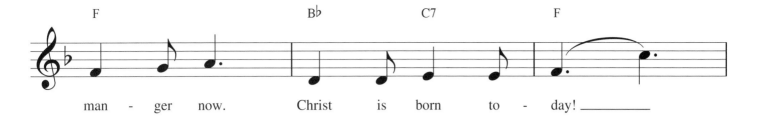

man - ger now. Christ is born to - day! _____

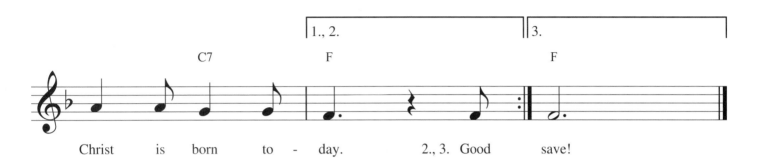

Christ is born to - day. 2., 3. Good save!

Additional Lyrics

2. Good Christian men, rejoice
   With heart and soul and voice.
   Now ye hear of endless bliss: Joy! Joy!
   Jesus Christ was born for this.
   He hath op'd the heavenly door,
   And man is blessed evermore.
   Christ was born for this!
   Christ was born for this!

3. Good Christian men, rejoice
   With heart and soul and voice.
   Now ye need not fear the grave: Peace! Peace!
   Jesus Christ was born to save!
   Calls you one and calls you all,
   To gain His everlasting hall.
   Christ was born to save!
   Christ was born to save!

Good King Wenceslas

Words by John M. Neale
Music from *Piae Cantiones*

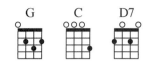

First note

Verse

Moderately, in 2

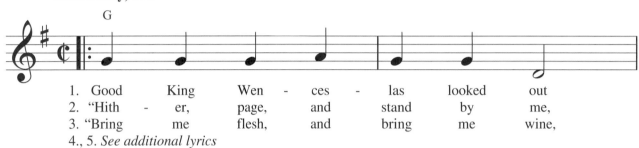

1. Good King Wen - ces - las looked out
2. "Hith - er, page, and stand by me,
3. "Bring me flesh, and bring me wine,
4., 5. *See additional lyrics*

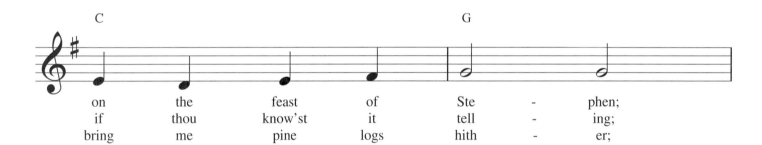

on the feast of Ste - phen;
if thou know'st it tell - ing;
bring me pine logs hith - er;

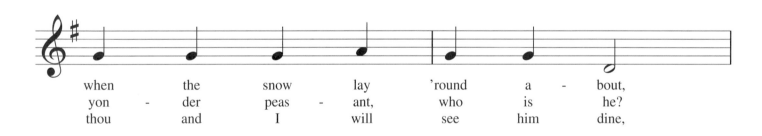

when the snow lay 'round a - bout,
yon - der peas - ant, who is he?
thou and I will see him dine,

deep and crisp and e - ven.
Where and what his dwell - ing?"
when we bear them thith - er."

Copyright © 2012 by HAL LEONARD CORPORATION
International Copyright Secured   All Rights Reserved

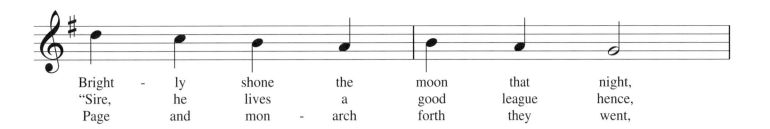

Bright - ly shone the moon that night,
"Sire, he lives a good league hence,
Page and mon - arch forth they went,

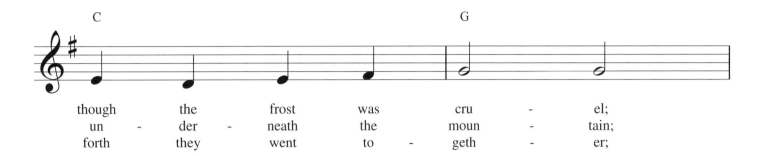

C   G

though the frost was cru - el;
un - der - neath the moun - tain;
forth they went to - geth - er;

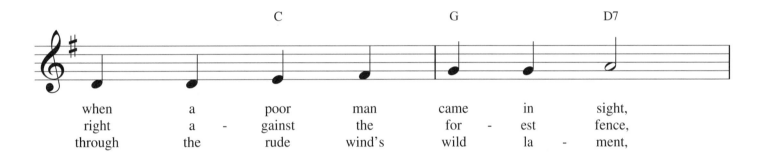

C   G   D7

when a poor man came in sight,
right a - gainst the for - est fence,
through the rude wind's wild la - ment,

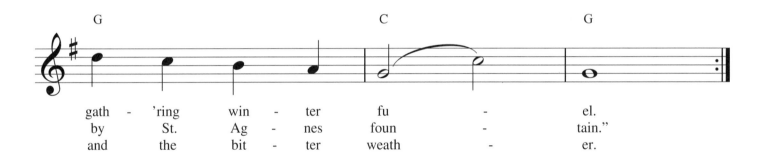

G   C   G

gath - 'ring win - ter fu - el.
by St. Ag - nes foun - tain."
and the bit - ter weath - er.

Additional Lyrics

4. "Sire, the night is darker now,
   And the wind blows stronger;
   Fails my heart, I know not how,
   I can go no longer."
   "Mark my footsteps, my good page,
   Tread thou in them boldly;
   Thou shalt find the winter's rage
   Freeze thy blood less coldly."

5. In his master's steps he trod,
   Where the snow lay dinted;
   Heat was in the very sod
   Which the saint has printed.
   Therefore, Christmas men, be sure,
   Wealth or rank possessing;
   Ye who now will bless the poor
   Shall yourselves find blessing.

He Is Born, the Holy Child

Traditional French Carol

First note

Chorus
Moderately, in 2

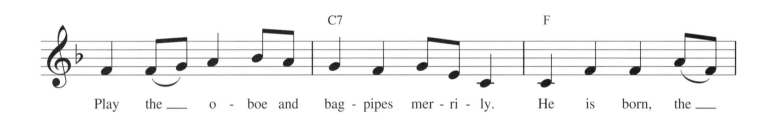

He is born, the ____ Ho - ly Child.

Play the ___ o - boe and bag - pipes mer - ri - ly. He is born, the ___

Fine

Ho - ly Child. Sing we all of the Sav - ior's birth.

Verse

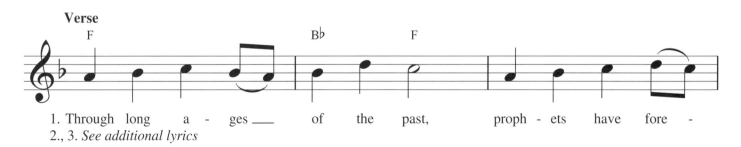

1. Through long a - ges ___ of the past, proph - ets have fore -
2., 3. *See additional lyrics*

Copyright © 2012 by HAL LEONARD CORPORATION
International Copyright Secured   All Rights Reserved

told His com - ing. Through long a - ges ____ of the past,

1., 2. | **3.**

D.C. al Fine

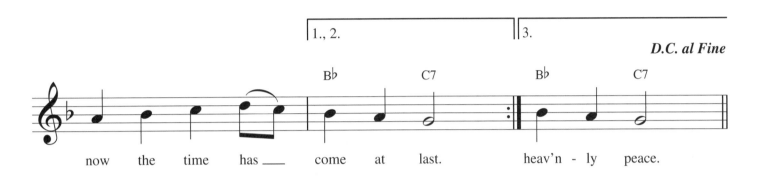

now the time has ____ come at last.　heav'n - ly peace.

Additional Lyrics

2. Oh, how lovely, oh, how pure,
   Is this perfect Child of heaven.
   Oh, how lovely, oh, how pure,
   Gracious gift of God to man.

3. Jesus, Lord of all the world,
   Coming as a child among us.
   Jesus, Lord of all the world,
   Grant to us Thy heav'nly peace.

Here We Come A-Wassailing

Traditional

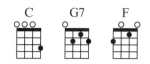

First note

Verse
Brightly

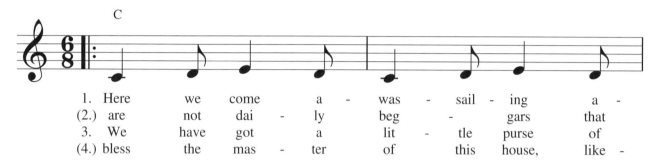

1. Here	we	come	a -	was	-	sail	ing	a -
(2.) are	not	dai -	ly	beg	-	gars		that
3. We	have	got	a	lit	-	tle	purse	of
(4.) bless	the	mas -	ter	of		this	house,	like -

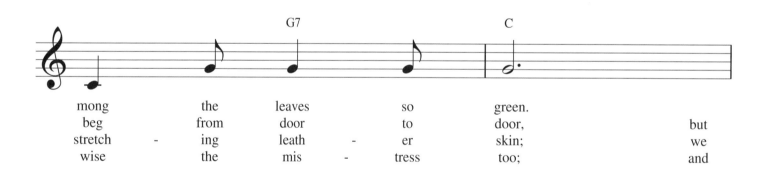

mong	the	leaves	so	green.		
beg	from	door	to	door,		but
stretch -	ing	leath -	er	skin;		we
wise	the	mis -	tress	too;		and

Here	we	come	a -	wan -	d'ring,	so	fair	to	be
we	are	neigh -	bor	chil -	dren	whom	you	have	seen	be -
want	a	lit -	tle	mon -	ey	to	line	the	well	with -
all	the	lit -	tle	chil -	dren	that	round	the	ta -	ble

Copyright © 2012 by HAL LEONARD CORPORATION
International Copyright Secured All Rights Reserved

Chorus

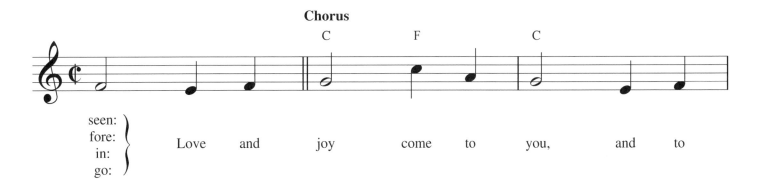

seen:
fore:
in:
go:

Love and joy come to you, and to

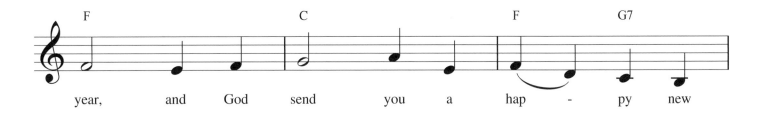

you your was - sail too. And God

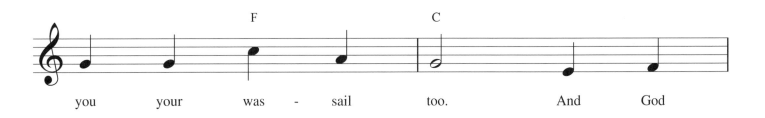

bless you, and send ____ you a hap - py new

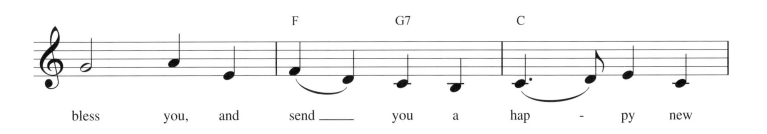

year, and God send you a hap - py new

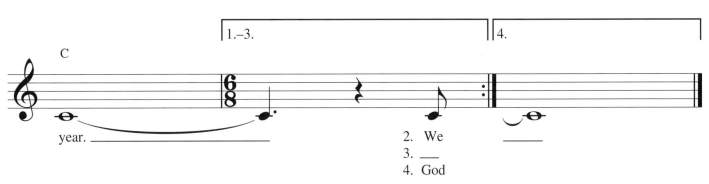

year. _____

1.–3.

4.

2. We

3. ___

4. God

The Holly and the Ivy

18th Century English Carol

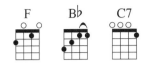

First note

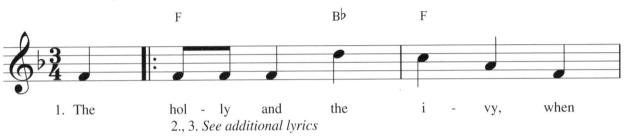

Verse
Moderately slow

1. The hol - ly and the i - vy, when
2., 3. See additional lyrics

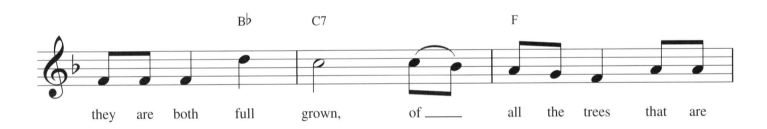

they are both full grown, of ___ all the trees that are

in the wood, the ___ hol - ly bears the crown. The

Copyright © 2012 by HAL LEONARD CORPORATION
International Copyright Secured   All Rights Reserved

Chorus

ris - ing of the sun _____ and the run - ning of the

deer, the ____ play - ing of the mer - ry or - gan, sweet

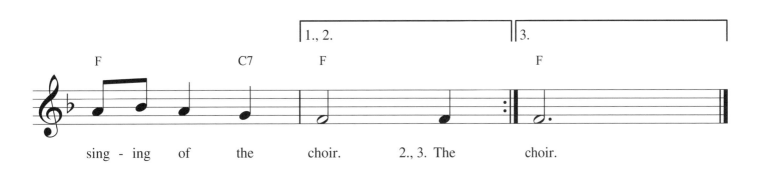

sing - ing of the choir. 2., 3. The choir.

Additional Lyrics

2. The holly bears a blossom,
   As white as lily flow'r,
   And Mary bore sweet Jesus Christ,
   To be our sweet Savior.

3. The holly bears a berry,
   As red as any blood,
   And Mary bore sweet Jesus Christ,
   To do poor sinners good.

I Saw Three Ships

Traditional English Carol

First note

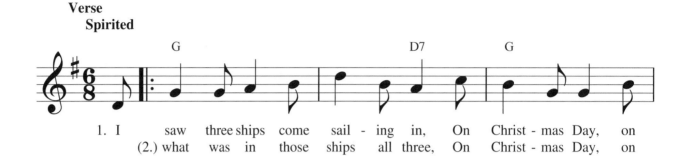

Verse
Spirited

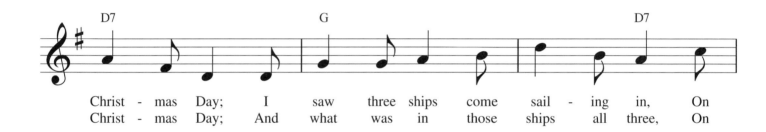

1. I saw three ships come sail-ing in, On Christ-mas Day, on
(2.) what was in those ships all three, On Christ-mas Day, on

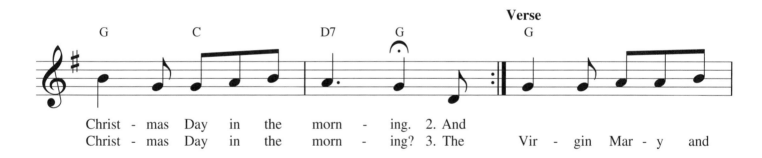

Christ-mas Day; I saw three ships come sail-ing in, On
Christ-mas Day; And saw what was in those ships all three, On

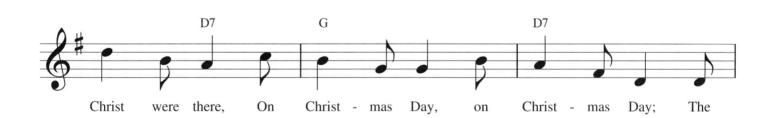

Christ-mas Day in the morn - ing. 2. And
Christ-mas Day in the morn - ing? 3. The Vir - gin Mar - y and

Christ were there, On Christ-mas Day, on Christ-mas Day; The

Vir - gin Mar - y and Christ were there, On Christ-mas Day in the morn - ing.

Copyright © 2012 by HAL LEONARD CORPORATION
International Copyright Secured   All Rights Reserved

Infant Holy, Infant Lowly

Traditional Polish Carol
Paraphrased by Edith M.G. Reed

Copyright © 2012 by HAL LEONARD CORPORATION
International Copyright Secured   All Rights Reserved

Jingle Bells

Words and Music by J. Pierpont

First note

Verse
Spirited, in 2

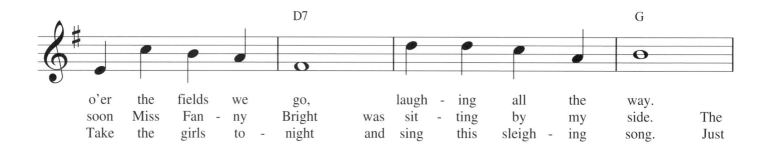

1. Dash - ing through the snow, in a one - horse o - pen sleigh,
(2.) day or two a - go, I thought I'd take a ride, and
3. Now the ground is white, go it while you're young.

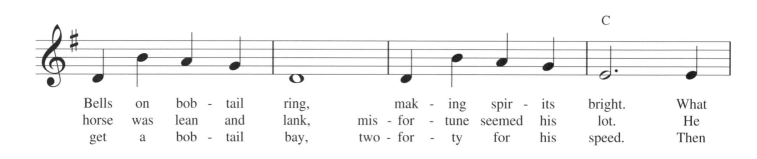

o'er the fields we go, laugh - ing all the way.
soon Miss Fan - ny Bright was sit - ting by my side. The
Take the girls to - night and sing this sleigh - ing song. Just

Bells on bob - tail ring, mak - ing spir - its bright. What
horse was lean and lank, mis - for - tune seemed his lot. He
get a bob - tail bay, two - for - ty for his speed. Then

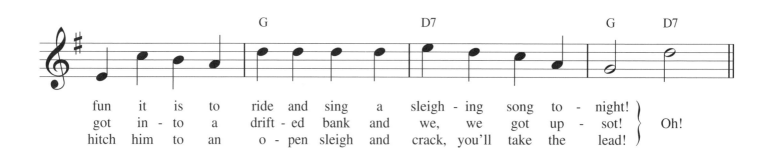

fun it is to ride and sing a sleigh - ing song to - night!
got in - to a drift - ed bank and we, we got up - sot! } Oh!
hitch him to an o - pen sleigh and crack, you'll take the lead!

Copyright © 2012 by HAL LEONARD CORPORATION
International Copyright Secured   All Rights Reserved

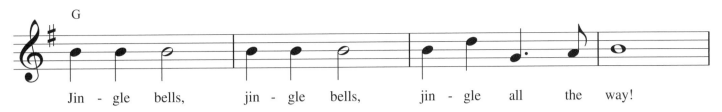

Jin - gle bells, jin - gle bells, jin - gle all the way!

Oh, what fun it is to ride in a one - horse o - pen sleigh! _____

Jin - gle bells, jin - gle bells, jin - gle all the

way! Oh, what fun it is to ride in a

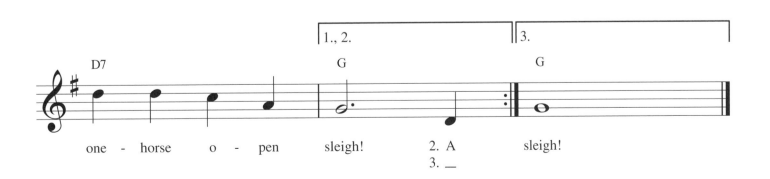

1., 2.   3.

one - horse o - pen sleigh!   2. A   sleigh!
                                                 3. _

Jolly Old St. Nicholas

Traditional 19th Century American Carol

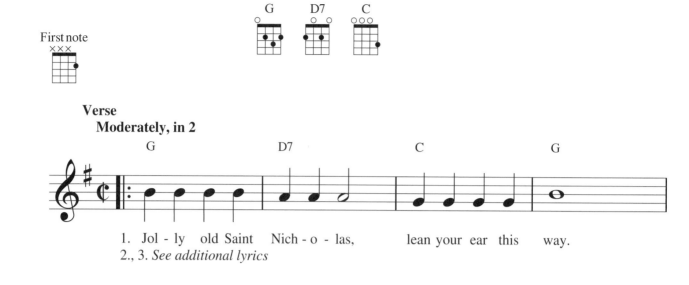

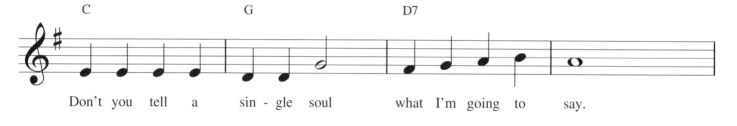

1. Jol - ly old Saint Nich - o - las, lean your ear this way.
2., 3. *See additional lyrics*

Don't you tell a sin - gle soul what I'm going to say.

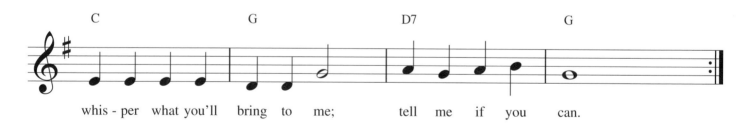

Christ-mas Eve is com - ing soon, now, you dear old man,

whis - per what you'll bring to me; tell me if you can.

Additional Lyrics

2. When the clock is striking twelve, when I'm fast asleep.
   Down the chimney broad and black, with your pack you'll creep.
   All the stockings you will find hanging in a row.
   Mine will be the shortest one, you'll be sure to know.

3. Johnny wants a pair of skates; Susy wants a sled.
   Nellie wants a picture book, yellow, blue and red.
   Now I think I'll leave to you what to give the rest.
   Choose for me, dear Santa Claus.
   You will know the best.

Copyright © 2012 by HAL LEONARD CORPORATION
International Copyright Secured   All Rights Reserved

Joy to the World

Words by Isaac Watts
Music by George Frideric Handel
Adapted by Lowell Mason

First note

Verse
Brightly

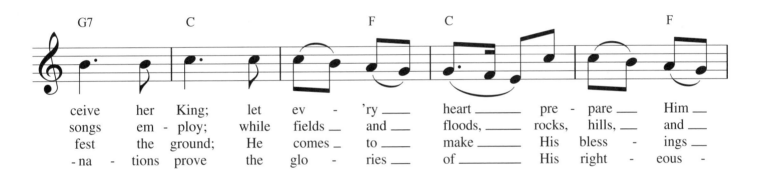

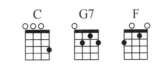

1. Joy to the world! The Lord is come; let earth re-
2. Joy to the world! The Sav - ior reigns; let men their
3. No more let sin and sor - row grow; nor thorns in -
4. He rules the world with truth and grace, and makes the

ceive her King; let ev - 'ry heart pre - pare Him
songs em - ploy; while fields and floods, rocks, hills, and
fest the ground; He comes to make His bless - ings
-na - tions prove the glo - ries of His right - eous -

room, and heav'n and na - ture sing, and heav'n and na - ture
plains re - peat the sound - ing joy, re - peat the sound - ing
flow, far as the curse is found, far as the curse is
ness, and won - ders of His love, and won - ders of His

sing, and heav'n and heav'n and na - ture sing.
joy, re - peat, re - peat the sound - ing joy.
found, far as, far as the curse is found.
love, and won - ders, and won - ders of His love.

Copyright © 2012 by HAL LEONARD CORPORATION
International Copyright Secured   All Rights Reserved

O Christmas Tree

Traditional German Carol

Copyright © 2012 by HAL LEONARD CORPORATION
International Copyright Secured   All Rights Reserved

O Come, All Ye Faithful

Music by John Francis Wade
Latin Words translated by Frederick Oakeley

First note

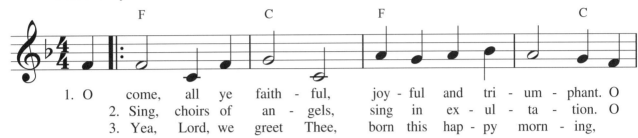

Verse
Moderately

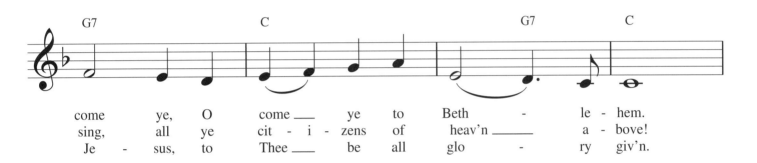

1. O come, all ye faith-ful, joy-ful and tri - um - phant. O
2. Sing, choirs of an - gels, sing in ex - ul - ta - tion. O
3. Yea, Lord, we greet Thee, born this hap - py morn - ing,

come ye, O come ___ ye to Beth - le - hem.
sing, all ye cit - i - zens of heav'n ___ a - bove!
Je - sus, to Thee ___ be all glo - ry giv'n.

Come and be - hold Him, born the King of an - gels. ⎫
Glo - ry to God, ___ in ___ the ___ high - est. ⎬ O
Word of the Fa - ther, now in flesh ap - pear - ing. ⎭

Chorus

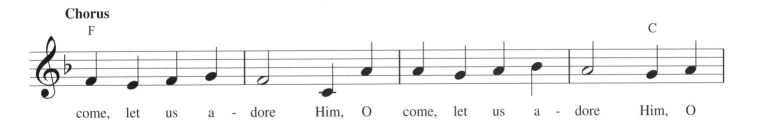

come, let us a - dore Him, O come, let us a - dore Him, O

come, let us a - dore Him, ___ Christ ___ the Lord!

Copyright © 2012 by HAL LEONARD CORPORATION
International Copyright Secured   All Rights Reserved

O Come, Little Children

Words by C. von Schmidt
Music by J.P.A. Schulz

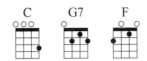

First note

Verse
Quietly

1. O come, lit - tle chil - dren, from cot and from
(2.) "Glo - ry to God!" sing the an - gels on

hall. O come to the man - ger in Beth - le - hem's stall. There
high, and "Peace up - on earth!" heav'n - ly voic - es re - ply. Then

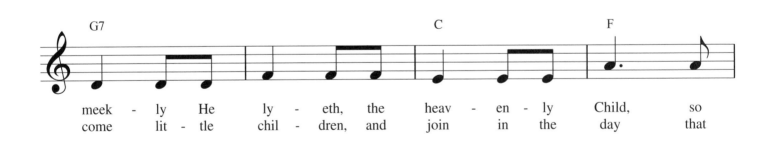

meek - ly He ly - eth, the heav - en - ly Child, so
come lit - tle chil - dren, and join in the day that

poor and so hum - ble, so sweet and so mild. 2. Now,
glad - ened the world on that first Christ-mas

Day.

Copyright © 2012 by HAL LEONARD CORPORATION
International Copyright Secured   All Rights Reserved

O Come, O Come, Immanuel

Plainsong, 13th Century
Words translated by John M. Neale and Henry S. Coffin

First note

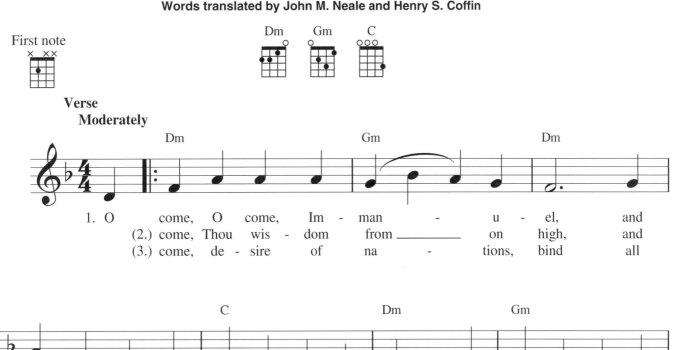

Verse
Moderately

1. O come, O come, Im - man - u - el, and
(2.) come, Thou wis - dom from _____ on high, and
(3.) come, de - sire of na - tions, bind all

ran - som cap - tive Is - ra - el, that mourns in lone - ly
or - der all things far _____ and nigh; to us the path of
peo - ple in one heart _____ and mind; bid en - vy, strife and

ex - ile here un - til the Son of God _____ ap -
knowl - edge show, and cause us in her ways _____ to
quar - rels cease; fill the whole world with heav - en's

Chorus

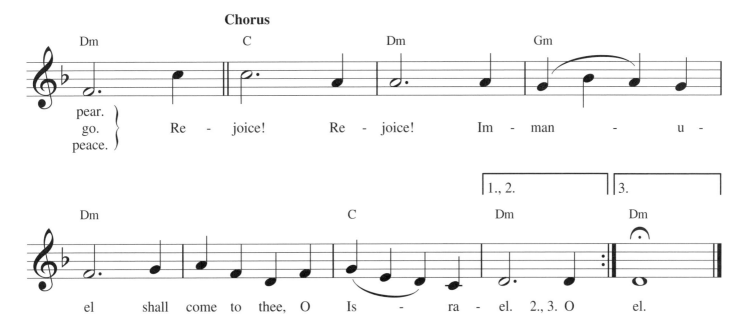

pear.
go.
peace.

Re - joice! Re - joice! Im - man - u -

1., 2.   3.

el shall come to thee, O Is - ra - el. 2., 3. O el.

Copyright © 2012 by HAL LEONARD CORPORATION
International Copyright Secured   All Rights Reserved

Once in Royal David's City

Words by Cecil F. Alexander
Music by Henry J. Gauntlett

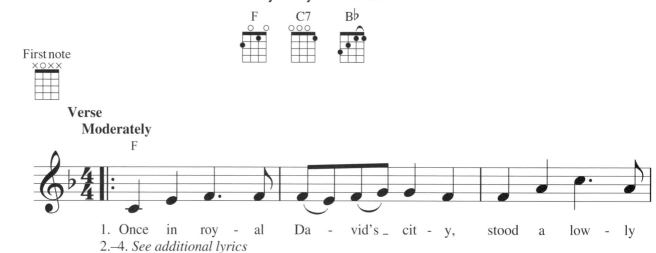

1. Once in roy - al Da - vid's cit - y, stood a low - ly
2.–4. *See additional lyrics*

cat - tle shed, where a moth - er laid her ba - by

in a man - ger for His bed. Mar - y was that

moth - er mild, Je - sus Christ her lit - tle child.

Additional Lyrics

2. He came down to earth from heaven,
Who is God and Lord of all,
And His shelter was a stable,
And His cradle was a stall.
With the poor, the mean and lowly,
Lived on earth our Savior holy.

3. Jesus is our childhood's pattern;
Day by day like us He grew.
He was little, weak and helpless;
Tears and smiles, like us, He knew.
And He feeleth for our sadness,
And He shareth in our gladness.

4. And our eyes at last shall see Him,
Through His own redeeming love,
For that child so dear and gentle
Is our Lord in heav'n above.
And He leads His children on
To the place where He is gone.

Copyright © 2012 by HAL LEONARD CORPORATION
International Copyright Secured   All Rights Reserved

Pat-A-Pan
(Willie, Take Your Little Drum)
Words and Music by Bernard de la Monnoye

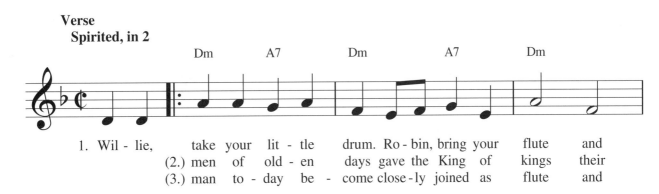

First note

Verse
Spirited, in 2

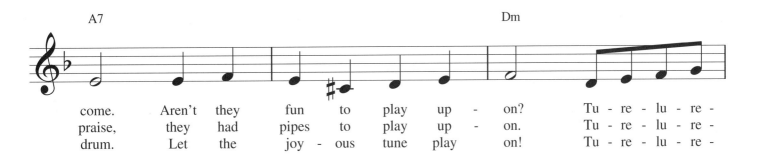

1. Wil - lie,   take your lit - tle drum. Ro - bin, bring your   flute   and
(2.) men   of old - en   days gave the King of   kings   their
(3.) man   to - day be - come close - ly joined as   flute   and

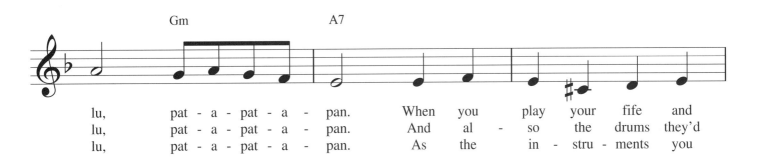

come.   Aren't they   fun   to   play up - on?   Tu - re - lu - re -
praise,   they had   pipes   to   play up - on.   Tu - re - lu - re -
drum.   Let the   joy - ous tune   play   on!   Tu - re - lu - re -

lu,   pat - a - pat - a - pan.   When   you   play your fife and
lu,   pat - a - pat - a - pan.   And   al - so   the drums they'd
lu,   pat - a - pat - a - pan.   As   the   in - stru - ments you

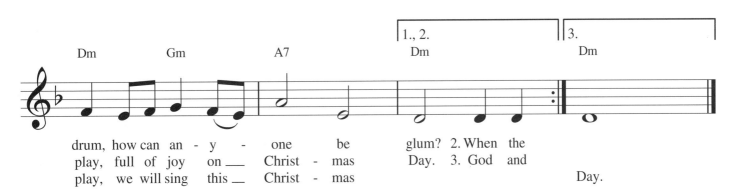

drum, how can an - y - one be   glum? 2. When the
play, full of joy on ___ Christ - mas   Day. 3. God and
play, we will sing this ___ Christ - mas
Day.

Copyright © 2012 by HAL LEONARD CORPORATION
International Copyright Secured   All Rights Reserved

Silent Night

Words by Joseph Mohr
Translated by John F. Young
Music by Franz X. Gruber

First note

Verse
Slowly

1. Si - lent night, ho - ly night! All is calm,
2. Si - lent night, ho - ly night! Shep - herds quake
3. Si - lent night, ho - ly night! Son of God,

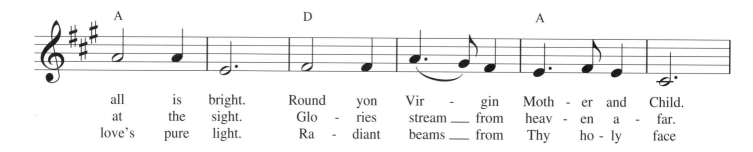

all is bright. Round yon Vir - gin Moth - er and Child.
at the sight. Glo - ries stream __ from heav - en a - far.
love's pure light. Ra - diant beams __ from Thy ho - ly face

Ho - ly In - fant so ten - der and mild, sleep in heav - en - ly
Heaven - ly hosts __ sing, Al - le - lu - ia. Christ the Sav - ior is
with the dawn of re - deem - ing grace. Je - sus, Lord, at Thy

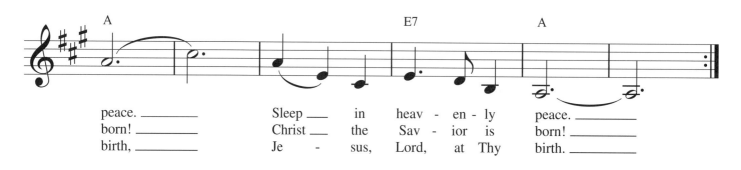

peace. _____ Sleep __ in heav - en - ly peace. _____
born! _____ Christ __ the Sav - ior is born! _____
birth, _____ Je - sus, Lord, at Thy birth. _____

Copyright © 2012 by HAL LEONARD CORPORATION
International Copyright Secured   All Rights Reserved

Up on the Housetop

Words and Music by B.R. Hanby

First note

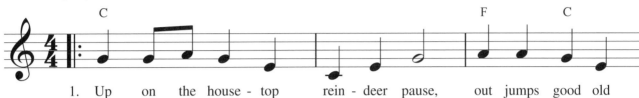

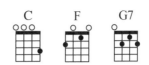

Verse
Brightly

1. Up on the house-top rein-deer pause, out jumps good old
2. First comes the stock-ing of lit-tle Nell. Oh, dear San-ta
3. Next comes the stock-ing of lit-tle Will. Oh, just see what a

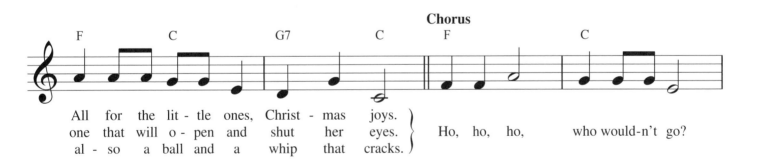

San-ta Claus. Down through the chim-ney with lots of toys.
fill it well. Give her a dol-ly that laughs and cries,
glo-rious fill! Here is a ham-mer and lots of tacks,

Chorus

All for the lit-tle ones, Christ-mas joys.
one that will o-pen and shut her eyes. } Ho, ho, ho, who would-n't go?
al-so a ball and a whip that cracks.

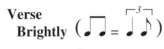

Ho, ho, ho, who would-n't go? _____ Up on the house-top,

click, click, click. Down through the chim-ney with good Saint Nick.

Copyright © 2012 by HAL LEONARD CORPORATION
International Copyright Secured   All Rights Reserved

While Shepherds Watched Their Flocks

Words by Nahum Tate
Music by George Frideric Handel

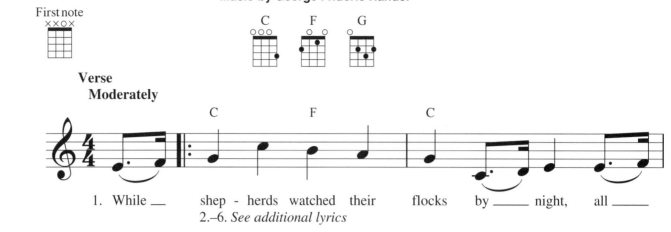

Verse
Moderately

1. While ___ shep - herds watched their flocks by ___ night, all ___
2.–6. *See additional lyrics*

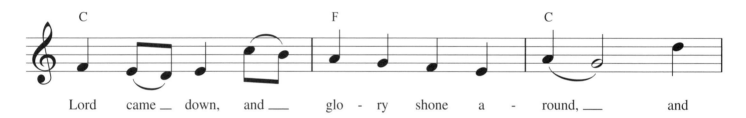

seat - ed on the ___ ground, ___ the ___ an - gel of the

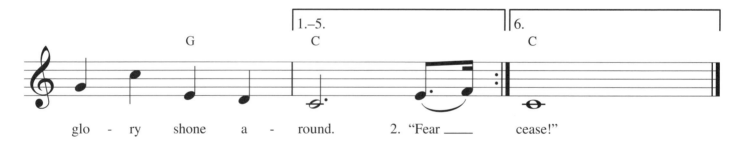

Lord came ___ down, and ___ glo - ry shone a - round, ___ and

glo - ry shone a - round. 2. "Fear ___ cease!"

Additional Lyrics

2. "Fear not!" said he, for mighty dread
   Had seized their troubled mind.
   "Glad tidings of great joy I bring
   To you and all mankind,
   To you and all mankind.

3. "To you, in David's town this day,
   Is born of David's line,
   The Savior, who is Christ the Lord;
   And this shall be the sign,
   And this shall be the sign:

4. "The heavenly Babe you there shall find
   To human view displayed,
   All meanly wrapped in swathing bands,
   And in a manger laid,
   And in a manger laid."

5. Thus spake the seraph; and forthwith
   Appeared a shining throng
   Of angels praising God on high,
   Who thus addressed their song,
   Who thus addressed their song:

6. "All glory be to God on high,
   And to the earth be peace;
   Good will henceforth from heav'n to men,
   Begin and never cease,
   Begin and never cease!"

Copyright © 2012 by HAL LEONARD CORPORATION
International Copyright Secured   All Rights Reserved

The Best Songs Ever

70 songs have now been arranged for ukulele. Includes: Always • Bohemian Rhapsody • Memory • My Favorite Things • Over the Rainbow • Piano Man • What a Wonderful World • Yesterday • You Raise Me Up • and more.

00282413 . . . . $17.99

Campfire Songs for Ukulele

30 favorites to sing as you roast marshmallows and strum your uke around the campfire. Includes: God Bless the U.S.A. • Hallelujah • The House of the Rising Sun • I Walk the Line • Puff the Magic Dragon • Wagon Wheel • You Are My Sunshine • and more.

00129170 . . . . $14.99

The Daily Ukulele

arr. Liz and Jim Beloff

Strum a different song everyday with easy arrangements of 365 of your favorite songs in one big songbook! Includes favorites by the Beatles, Beach Boys, and Bob Dylan, folk songs, pop songs, kids' songs, Christmas carols, and Broadway and Hollywood tunes, all with a spiral binding for ease of use.

00240356 Original Edition $39.99
00240681 Leap Year Edition $39.99
00119270 Portable Edition $37.50

Disney Hits for Ukulele

Play 23 of your favorite Disney songs on your ukulele. Includes: The Bare Necessities • Cruella De Vil • Do You Want to Build a Snowman? • Kiss the Girl • Lava • Let It Go • Once upon a Dream • A Whole New World • and more.

00151250 . . . . $16.99

Also available:

00291547 **Disney Fun Songs for Ukulele** . . . $16.99
00701708 **Disney Songs for Ukulele** $14.99
00334696 **First 50 Disney Songs on Ukulele** . $16.99

First 50 Songs You Should Play on Ukulele

An amazing collec-tion of 50 accessible, must-know favorites: Edelweiss • Hey, Soul Sister • I Walk the Line • I'm Yours • Imagine • Over the Rainbow • Peaceful Easy Feeling • The Rainbow Connection • Riptide • more.

00149250 . . . . $16.99

Also available:

00292082 **First 50 Melodies on Ukulele** . . . $15.99
00289029 **First 50 Songs on Solo Ukulele** . . $15.99
00347437 **First 50 Songs to Strum on Uke** . $16.99

40 Most Streamed Songs for Ukulele

40 top hits that sound great on uke! Includes: Despacito • Feel It Still • Girls like You • Happier • Havana • High Hopes • The Middle • Perfect • 7 Rings • Shallow • Shape of You • Something Just like This • Stay • Sucker • Sunflower • Sweet but Psycho • Thank U, Next • There's Nothing Holdin' Me Back • Without Me • and more!

00298113 . . . . $17.99

The 4 Chord Songbook

With just 4 chords, you can play 50 hot songs on your ukulele! Songs include: Brown Eyed Girl • Do Wah Diddy Diddy • Hey Ya! • Ho Hey • Jessie's Girl • Let It Be • One Love • Stand by Me • Toes • With or Without You • and many more.

00142050 . . . . $16.99

Also available:

00141143 **The 3-Chord Songbook** $16.99

Pop Songs for Kids

30 easy pop favorites for kids to play on uke, including: Brave • Can't Stop the Feeling! • Feel It Still • Fight Song • Happy • Havana • House of Gold • How Far I'll Go • Let It Go • Remember Me (Ernesto de la Cruz) • Rewrite the Stars • Roar • Shake It Off • Story of My Life • What Makes You Beautiful • and more.

00284415 . . . . $16.99

Simple Songs for Ukulele

50 favorites for standard G-C-E-A ukulele tuning, including: All Along the Watchtower • Can't Help Falling in Love • Don't Worry, Be Happy • Ho Hey • I'm Yours • King of the Road • Sweet Home Alabama • You Are My Sunshine • and more.

00156815 . . . . $14.99

Also available:

00276644 **More Simple Songs for Ukulele** . $14.99

Top Hits of 2020

18 uke-friendly tunes of 2020 are featured in this collection of melody, lyric and chord arrangements in standard G-C-E-A tuning. Includes: Adore You (Harry Styles) • Before You Go (Lewis Capaldi) • Cardigan (Taylor Swift) • Daisies (Katy Perry) • I Dare You (Kelly Clarkson) • Level of Concern (twenty one pilots) • No Time to Die (Billie Eilish) • Rain on Me (Lady Gaga feat. Ariana Grande) • Say So (Doja Cat) • and more.

00355553 . . . . $14.99

Also available:

00302274 **Top Hits of 2019** $14.99

Ukulele: The Most Requested Songs

Strum & Sing Series
Cherry Lane Music

Nearly 50 favorites all expertly arranged for ukulele! Includes: Bubbly • Build Me Up, Buttercup • Cecilia • Georgia on My Mind • Kokomo • L-O-V-E • Your Body Is a Wonderland • and more.

02501453 . . . . $14.99

The Ultimate Ukulele Fake Book

Uke enthusiasts will love this giant, spiral-bound collection of over 400 songs for uke! Includes: Crazy • Dancing Queen • Downtown • Fields of Gold • Happy • Hey Jude • 7 Years • Summertime • Thinking Out Loud • Thriller • Wagon Wheel • and more.

00175500 9" x 12" Edition $45.00
00319997 5.5" x 8.5" Edition $39.99

Order today from your favorite music retailer at
halleonard.com

Prices, contents and availability subject to change without notice

Disney characters and artwork TM & © 2021 Disney

HAL•LEONARD® UKULELE PLAY-ALONG

Now you can play your favorite songs on your uke with great-sounding backing tracks to help you sound like a bona fide pro! The audio also features playback tools so you can adjust the tempo without changing the pitch and loop challenging parts.

1. POP HITS
00701451 Book/CD Pack $15.99

3. HAWAIIAN FAVORITES
00701453 Book/Online Audio $14.99

4. CHILDREN'S SONGS
00701454 Book/Online Audio $14.99

5. CHRISTMAS SONGS
00701696 Book/CD Pack $12.99

6. LENNON & MCCARTNEY
00701723 Book/Online Audio $12.99

7. DISNEY FAVORITES
00701724 Book/Online Audio $14.99

8. CHART HITS
00701745 Book/CD Pack $15.99

9. THE SOUND OF MUSIC
00701784 Book/CD Pack $14.99

10. MOTOWN
00701964 Book/CD Pack $12.99

11. CHRISTMAS STRUMMING
00702458 Book/Online Audio $12.99

12. BLUEGRASS FAVORITES
00702584 Book/CD Pack $12.99

13. UKULELE SONGS
00702599 Book/CD Pack $12.99

14. JOHNNY CASH
00702615 Book/Online Audio $15.99

15. COUNTRY CLASSICS
00702834 Book/CD Pack $12.99

16. STANDARDS
00702835 Book/CD Pack $12.99

17. POP STANDARDS
00702836 Book/CD Pack $12.99

18. IRISH SONGS
00703086 Book/Online Audio $12.99

19. BLUES STANDARDS
00703087 Book/CD Pack $12.99

20. FOLK POP ROCK
00703088 Book/CD Pack $12.99

21. HAWAIIAN CLASSICS
00703097 Book/CD Pack $12.99

22. ISLAND SONGS
00703098 Book/CD Pack $12.99

23. TAYLOR SWIFT
00221966 Book/Online Audio $16.99

24. WINTER WONDERLAND
00101871 Book/CD Pack $12.99

25. GREEN DAY
00110398 Book/CD Pack $14.99

26. BOB MARLEY
00110399 Book/Online Audio $14.99

27. TIN PAN ALLEY
00116358 Book/CD Pack $12.99

28. STEVIE WONDER
00116736 Book/CD Pack $14.99

29. OVER THE RAINBOW & OTHER FAVORITES
00117076 Book/Online Audio $15.99

30. ACOUSTIC SONGS
00122336 Book/CD Pack $14.99

31. JASON MRAZ
00124166 Book/CD Pack $14.99

32. TOP DOWNLOADS
00127507 Book/CD Pack $14.99

33. CLASSICAL THEMES
00127892 Book/Online Audio $14.99

34. CHRISTMAS HITS
00128602 Book/CD Pack $14.99

35. SONGS FOR BEGINNERS
00129009 Book/Online Audio $14.99

36. ELVIS PRESLEY HAWAII
00138199 Book/Online Audio $14.99

37. LATIN
00141191 Book/Online Audio $14.99

38. JAZZ
00141192 Book/Online Audio $14.99

39. GYPSY JAZZ
00146559 Book/Online Audio $15.99

40. TODAY'S HITS
00160845 Book/Online Audio $14.99

HAL•LEONARD®

www.halleonard.com

Prices, contents, and availability subject to change without notice.

1021
483